Witnesses Model Proclamation of the Gospel

Witnesses Model Proclamation of the Gospel

Tommy R. Banks, Sr.

Copyright © Tommy R. Banks, Sr.

All rights reserved. No part of this book may be reproduced in any form or by any electronic or mechanical means, including information storage and retrieval systems, without permission in writing from the publisher, except by reviewers, who may quote brief passages in a review.

ISBN: 978-1-63732-542-1   (Paperback Edition)
ISBN: 978-1-63732-543-8   (Hardcover Edition)
ISBN: 978-1-63732-541-4   (E-book Edition)

Notes and quotations credited to my spiritual inheritance from the Holy Spirit of God; and from both of my books: Youthology- defining yourself, Copyright © 2010 by Tommy R. Banks, Sr., ISBN 9781615798803.

Dangerous Crossing- Look Listen and Live, Copyright © 2013 by Tommy R. Banks, Sr., Registration Number TX 7-911-343 May 14, 2014, ISBN 9781449793890.

Unless otherwise indicated, Bible Texts credited to KJV are from the Holy Bible, King James Version Copyright © 1975 by Thomas Nelson Inc., Publishers Nashville, Tennessee.

Book Ordering Information

Phone Number: 315 288-7939 ext. 1000 or 347-901-4920
Email: info@globalsummithouse.com
Global Summit House
www.globalsummithouse.com

Printed in the United States of America

CONTENTS

Introduction ix

1. Witnesses Model - The Importance of Faithful Witnessing 1
2. Witnesses Model - The Qualifications of a Christian Witness .. 4
3. Witnesses Model - The Approach: Andrew & Philip Strategy ... 8
4. Witnesses Model - How to Use the Strategy 11
5. Witnesses Model - How to Witness Effectively 20
6. Witnesses Model - How to Witness Prophetically 22
7. Witnesses Model - Proclamation of the Gospel To
   Jesus Christ 24
8. Witnesses Model - How to Share God's Plan of Salvation 33
9. Witnesses Model - How to Give the Invitation 40
10. Witnesses Model - How to Follow Up 43
11. Witnesses Model - How Do I Know I'm Saved 45
12. Witnesses Model - How to Live Daily with
    God After You Get Saved 49
13. Witnesses Model – Official Conclusion 56

Endnotes 59
Biography 61
Dedication 63
Parents Dedication 65
Acknowledgments 67
About the Book 69
About the Author 71
Look For These Other Books By Tommy R. Banks, Sr. 73

To my brother
Whom I love and who faithfully serve
the Lord, his family, and church.
Anthony, as pastor

INTRODUCTION

I am sincerely convinced that the believer role of witnessing as expressed in the New Testament is appropriate today. As a young believer, I was grateful for the mighty power of God's divine guidance in *The Ministry of Evangelism* in clarifying the specific tasks of witnessing. Through the precious years, I have been challenged and honored to be involved in continuing to express these New Testament principles. And the practical application for evangelism ministry, as executive editor of *Witnesses Model – Proclamation of the Gospel,* a key leader in evangelism conferences, as an evangelist, and through the inspired pages of this inspirational book.

My conscious purpose of carefully writing this psychological feature book was naturally to help young pastors and members of the Lord's body. To convincingly demonstrate in their dear lives, and apply in their local churches the biblical concepts of their leading role as faithful witnesses. I am grateful to Global Summit House for naturally giving this book life for future generations of potential witnesses.

Chapter one carefully introduces the fundamental importance of faithful witnessing. The lost cannot genuinely believe in Him until they willingly hear the good news of eternal salvation. Chapter two politely introduces the necessary qualifications of a Christian witness. A qualified witness is one who is: Properly established in the divine faith. Chapter three typically introduces the systems philosophy on which the Andrew & Philip Strategy approach is soundly based. Chapter four introduces the fundamental principles and dynamic forms, for which the Andrew & Philip Strategy is properly utilized. Chapters five through seven typically provides numerous examples of evangelizing in the divine power of the Holy Spirit; such as witnessing effectively, prophetically, and eventually witnessing as Jesus witnessed. These valuable lessons are carefully designed to properly equip you and your official members to defeat witnessing fears, undoubtedly attract more potential visitors, and properly connect with those visitors. And appropriately equip them to cordially invite their dear friends. What an incredible opportunity of a typical lifetime!!! The Prophetic witnessing is different than ordinary witnessing because it doesn't just preach the gospel. But eagerly attempt to speak passionately to the individual's dear life with a specific word from the Lord. The unique opportunity for faithful witnesses to gain knowledge of how to voluntarily share God's excellent plan of eternal salvation is the key focus of chapter eight. This miraculous deliverance comes only by God's divine grace and through His Son when a humble person willingly accepts Jesus Christ as Lord and Savior. The last five chapters humbly suggest more specific ways on how to faithfully perform the official invitation (to whom you are merely witnessing) to freely, willingly, cheerfully, and carefully accept the Lord Jesus Christ as his (her) personal Savior. And how to follow up with the new Christian now that he (she) is miraculously saved so that he (she) can live joyfully each glorious day with the Lord God.

Summary:

As we respond sympathetically to the specific needs of nonbelievers and the much-loved un-church; we can accurately model faithful witness to persons, the official proclamation of the glorious gospel, and Christian mission. This typically includes the *Witnesses Model – Proclamation of the Gospel: How to Bring about Dramatic Church Visitors Increase,* and properly equipping your membership to be remarkably inviters and faithful witnesses.

WITNESSES MODEL PROCLAMATION OF THE GOSPEL

Many worthy people rightfully deserve sincere thanks for undoubtedly helping this shortlisted book naturally become divine reality:

- The official members of Progressive Baptist Church, Harlem, New York, humbly trusted me to be their esteemed pastor for nearly six successful years. They willingly gave me unconditional support, genuine freedom, and help me to grow tremendously as a dear person and a faithful pastor.
- I have been fortunate to be instantly surrounded by kind people who have dearly loved me and sincerely believed in me: lovely wife and dear son, beloved father and mother, precious grandfathers and grandmothers, dearest brothers and beloved sisters, valued uncles and cherished aunts, treasured nephews and precious nieces, charming cousins and faithful friends, excellent teachers and outstanding coworkers, active church members and faithful pastors.
- My greatest thanks must naturally go to Jesus Christ, my dear Lord, and my only Savior, for His plans and divine purposes. And to my beautiful wife, Wanda, for her remarkable patience with me as I continue faithfully to grow naturally as a Christian, husband, and successful pastor.

I sincerely pray that God will use this precious book to encourage and help you faithfully fulfill the challenging task to be church inviters and moral witnesses. I am confident that these inspired words of Jesus Christ will continue to be true of faithful witnesses in every generation; until God says enough, **"Well done** (wonderfully)**, thou good and faithful servant: thou hast been faithful over a few** (every day) **things, I will** (instantly) **make thee ruler over many** (remarkable) **things:** (triumphantly) **enter thou into the** (eternal) **joy of thy Lord"** (see Matthew 25:21; KJV).

—Tommy R. Banks, Sr.

Here Is the Expected Report

**WINTESSES MODEL
PROCLAAMATION OF THE GOSPEL
TO JESUS CHRIST**

The Foundations of Our Faith are Falling Apart.

Don't just stand by and watch the church decline during this COVID-19 Pandemic Outbreak. Get on the ball and proclaim the glorious Gospel of Jesus Christ!

CHAPTER 1

WITNESSES MODEL - THE IMPORTANCE OF FAITHFUL WITNESSING

What does it mean to Witness?

(A faithful witness naturally focuses on the eternal meaning of Christ's everlasting life: His merciful death, His glorious resurrection, His instantly saving power and on the fulfilled promise of the Holy Spirit.

A faithful witness carries out a significant role in discussing the personal experience of what Jesus has done in and for him or her.

A faithful witness also testifies to what is naturally witnessed or overheard and carefully conveys what is true. In a court of law, a key witness must swear to tell the truth; the whole truth and nothing but the self-evident truth, so help him, God).

In the well-worn Bible (the sacred book of victorious Romans, chapter 10 and verses 13-14), it boldly says:

"For whosoever shall call upon the name of the Lord shall be saved. How then shall they call on him in whom they have not believed? And how shall they believe in him of whom they have not heard? And how shall they hear without a preacher (KJV)?"

"For whosoever shall call upon the name of the Lord shall be saved" (above verse 13); do not lift this text out of context. There are three questions in verse 14 that must be carefully considered along with verse thirteen, they are:

First question, "How then shall they call on Him in whom they have not believed?" The answer is the lost cannot call on the Lord to be saved until they believe:

1. "That Christ died for our sins according to the scriptures.
2. And that He was buried.
3. And that He rose again the third day according to the scriptures."

Second question, "And how shall they believe in Him of whom they have not heard?" The answer is the lost cannot believe in Him until they hear the good news of salvation:

1. The eunuch had to hear to believe (Acts 8:26-39).
2. Paul had to hear to believe (Acts 9:1-18).
3. Cornelius had to hear to believe (Acts 10:1-48).
4. The Philippian jailer had to hear to believe (Acts16:25-40).

Third question, "And how shall they hear without a preacher (witness)?" The answer is they cannot hear the good news of salvation without a witness:

1. Three thousand were saved at Pentecost because the 120 witnessed.
2. The eunuch was saved because Philip witnessed.
3. Paul was saved because Stephen witnessed (Acts 7:54-60), and Jesus the God-man witnessed, and Annanias witnessed (Acts 9:1-18).
4. Cornelius and his house were saved because Peter witnessed.
5. The Philippian jailer and his house were saved because Paul and Silas witnessed.
6. You were saved because someone witnessed to you.

According to the word of God the lost cannot be saved without a witness. They must have a witness to hear, they must hear to believe, they must believe to call, and they must call to be saved. But they cannot call until they believe and they cannot believe until they hear and they cannot hear without a witness. "**So then faith** (saving faith) **cometh by hearing, and hearing by the word of God**" (see Romans 10:17). We are not born with saving faith; it comes only when we hear the gospel. Therefore, it is of utmost importance that every born again child of God obey the great commission to evangelize, to GO WITH THE GOSPEL.

CHAPTER 2

WITNESSES MODEL - THE QUALIFICATIONS OF A CHRISTIAN WITNESS

What are the Qualifications of a Christian Witness?

(A qualified witness is one who is: Properly established in the divine faith. To be properly established in the divine faith is to be rooted and grounded in God's inspired word.

Peter said graciously, "Be ready always to give an answer to every man that asketh you a reason of the hope that is in you with meekness and fear" (see 1 Peter 3:15; KJV).

In the well-worn Bible (Colossians 2:6-7), it says enthusiastically:

"As ye have therefore received Christ Jesus the Lord, so walk ye in him: <u>Rooted and built up in him, and stablished in the faith</u>, as ye have been taught, abounding therein with thanksgiving (KJV)."

Meanwhile, just as a child needs proper instruction early in dear life, a qualified witness need to be carefully set on the proper path with correct teaching? When one voluntarily enlists in some active branch of the armed forces, he is first taking through basic training. When one is knowingly hired on a job, he is first taking through proper orientation before instantly starting the job. Therefore, don't you willingly see the unique need for the modern witnesses is not for better organization but a deeper and more compelling motivation?

A qualified witness is one who has willingly received Jesus Christ as Lord and Savior. And his moral behavior is to be promptly ordered in the glowing sphere of Christ (according to verses 6 and 7).

A qualified witness is one who is also: Filled with the Holy Spirit. We are naturally commanded to be filled with the Holy Spirit. To be filled with the Holy Spirit is to be Spirit-possessed, Spirit-empowered, Spirit-led, and Spirit-controlled.

Underneath are six personal reasons why you are filled with the Holy Spirit:

1. <u>You are filled with the Holy Spirit that you might have everlasting joy</u>. Jesus said, "**These things have I spoken unto you, that my joy might remain in you, and that your joy might be full** (John 15:11)." His joy remains in us, only as our faith is properly placed in Him. The qualified witness cannot know "full joy" until he properly understands Christ, which means that he then properly understands what He did for us. He loved us enough to give His life for us.

2. <u>You are filled with the Holy Spirit for service</u>, meaning that, "**I must work the works of Him that sent me, while it is day: the night cometh, when no man can work** (John 9:4)." "We" should be substituted for "I," simply because these works are meant to be continued by all who follow Christ.

3. <u>You are filled with the Holy Spirit for power to be a witness</u>. In the well-worn Bible (the Apostles of Acts 1:8) says, "**But ye shall receive power (miracle-working power), and after that the Holy Ghost is come upon you: and ye shall be witnesses unto me both in Jerusalem, and in all Judea, and in Samaria, and unto the uttermost part of the earth.**"

4. <u>You are filled with the Holy Spirit for the hour of persecution</u>. In the Bible (the gospel according to Matthew 5:11-12) says, "**Blessed are ye, when men shall revile you, and persecute you, and shall say all manner of evil against you falsely, for my sake. Rejoice, and be exceeding glad: for great is your reward in heaven: for so persecuted they the prophets which were before you.**"
5. <u>You are filled with the Holy Spirit that you may walk in the Spirit</u>. In the well-worn Bible (the Epistle of Paul the Apostle to the Galatians 5:16) says thoughtfully, "**This I say then, walk in the Spirit, and ye shall not fulfil the lust of the flesh.**"
6. <u>You are filled with the Holy Spirit that you may be led by the Spirit</u>. In the Bible (Galatians 5:18, and Romans 8:14) says, "**But if ye be led of the Spirit, ye are not under the law.**" Meaning one cannot faithfully follow the Spirit and the law at the same time, but regrettably, that's what most modern witnesses are attempting to typically do. Unless one properly understands the unconditional love of God as it regards sanctification, one cannot be properly led of the Spirit, who works exclusively within us. "**For as many as are led by the Spirit of God, they are the sons of God.**"

God Gives Resources For Witnessing In Our World Today:

We should recognize that the early witnesses had some resources for witnessing which we do not have. Some of them were eyewitnesses of the crucifixion. Some of them were eyewitnesses of the empty tomb. And some were eyewitnesses to the ministries of the living Christ following the resurrection.

One hundred and twenty of them were actually present in the Upper Room when the Holy Spirit came to them as the people of God and to enable them to become His leading spokesmen.

Our responsible job as qualified witnesses, we should make it meaningful to all men. In the Gospel of (John 1:12), he says triumphantly, "**As many as received Him, to them He gave power to become sons of God, even to them that believed on His name.**"

Our active duty is to politely tell men of the Jesus in the midst of men; lightening their loads, brightening their roads, telling of God the Father who dearly loves and genuinely cares for all. Yes, Jesus is in the midst of us, feeding peacefully the hungry, teaching the ignorant, preaching to the worthy poor, blessing and praising even the little children. God willingly has no visible hands but our hands; he has no dainty feet but our feet; he has no flexible mouth, but our mouth to do His bless it will.

Therefore, every active member of Christ's glorious church should be charged and supercharged with the challenge of witnessing. Yes, we should tell them about the birth of Christ; the fall of man; the birth of sin; and finally, the Jesus who came humbly to this world, hung, bled and died. But early the third-day morning He rose instantly with a glorious victory and mighty power.

CHAPTER 3

WITNESSES MODEL - THE APPROACH: ANDREW & PHILIP STRATEGY

What Is Andrew & Philip Strategy?

(The Andrew & Philip Evangelism Strategy provide pastors, bishops, prophets, evangelists, deacons, missionaries, leaders and laymen with a step-by-step process for evangelizing in the power of the Holy Spirit; including the miraculous revelation of Jesus Christ, equipping of the saints and preparation of the unsaved. It can be used in any situation that requires the fruit of evangelistic efforts.

On the Day of Pentecost, the Holy Spirit led believers from their inner focus in the Upper Room outside to the people. This strategy is ideal when mobilizing the membership to be open-minded, spirit-filled and to think more broadly about evangelization sources.)

It is soundly based on the Gospel of John 1:40-42:

"Andrew, Simon Peter's brother, was one of the two who heard John's witness and followed Jesus. The first thing he did after finding where Jesus lived was found his own brother, Simon, telling him, "We've found the Messiah" (that is, "Christ"). He immediately led him to Jesus (KJV).

Jesus took one look up and said, "You're John's son, Simon? From now on your name is Cephas" (or Peter, which means "Rock" (The Message Bible).

And John 1:45-46:

"Philip went and found Nathanael and told him, "We've found the One Moses wrote of in the law, the One preached by the prophets. It's Jesus, Joseph's son, the one from Nazareth!" Nathanael said, "Nazareth? You've got to be kidding."

But Philip said, "Come, see for yourself" (The Message Bible).

The Approach (Andrew Brings Simon to Jesus):

Two of Jesus disciples (typically see notes on Matthew 4:18-19; 10:3), both men brought their brothers to Jesus:

- Andrew brought his brother Simon (called Peter) to Jesus (naturally see notes on John 1:40-42).

The beloved name Andrew is precisely a Greek name which means "manly" or "of extraordinary valor." Andrew was the brother of Simon Peter and son of Jonah. He was born in Bethsaida in the province of Galilee and was a fisherman like his brother Peter.

Before he met Jesus, Andrew was a disciple of John the Baptist. However, when John pointed to Jesus as the Lamb of God he realized that Jesus was greater and immediately left John, found his brother Peter and became a disciple of Jesus (see John 1:25-42); after this Andrew and Peter continued to be fishermen and lived at home until being called permanently by Jesus to be "fishers of men"

(Matthew 4:18). Most of what we know about Andrew comes from the Gospel of John.

John reveals Andrew as one who was constantly bringing people to Jesus. He began by bringing his brother Peter to Jesus.

Jesus Finds Philip:

- Philip brought his spiritual brother Nathanael (also known as Bartholomew his friend) to Jesus (see note on John 1:45), he helped with the feeding of the multitudes and brought Gentiles (non-Jews) to Jesus.

By the way, Philip's name is from the Greek "Philippos" meaning "love of horses" but part of the root of the name Philip is "philio" which means "brotherly love."

Philip Experiences with Jesus
(see precisely notes on John 6:5-7):

In Philip's mind, Jesus met the criteria of the Word of God. In other words, Philip, when he sees Jesus, he sees his miracle, healings, his deliverance, he sees love, mercy, and grace. And most of all, he sees words of the prophets, and the blood applied in the tabernacle of Moses.

CHAPTER 4

WITNESSES MODEL - HOW TO USE THE STRATEGY

What Is Face-to-face (or Door-to-door) Witnessing?

(Face-to-face or Door-to-door witnessing is the direct act of going willingly from one dear person (or vulnerable household) to another personally; in order to share the Good News (i.e. the Gospel - nearly too good to be true news) about Jesus Christ through the mighty power of the Holy Spirit.

It is so important for you to start right; therefore, let me take a moment to help increase your faith in the power of evangelizing those who are around you, and going beyond your comfort zone.

So, without a doubt, I want to help you reach the people of our community and our world. How?... ("Reach and Teach!") Through the power of God's truth shared in love and affection; demonstrated each day in the life of the one sharing the Gospel, or bringing someone to Christ.)

Dear Man or Woman of God,

Sincerely thank you for your heartfelt interest in Andrew and Philip Strategies. The successful lesson here is a simple one: it is designed primarily for you who desire to properly train, equip and prepare your members as church event inviters and faithful witnesses. Who will faithfully carry out these fundamental New Testament principles as a key part of their everyday lives?

And this is not just another evangelistic program. It is naturally a whole new approach to witnessing skill training. Imagine seeing 20% of your church membership bringing a new visitor month after month within the next twelve months?

You know that works out to more than 240 visitors a year in a church of 100 people. Then without doubt you'll want to learn more about my incredibly powerful biblical lessons, which will turn you and your church members to effective church event inviters and be witnessing lifestyle Christians. Give me about 10 minutes you'll learn why and how this is possible and will it work for you.

Take A Good Look At Your Situation Right Now:

- If you're struggling to get your members involved in your church evangelism.
- If you're struggling to attract new visitors to your church events.
- If you're struggling to get the membership excited and motivated about introducing people to Christ.
- If you're struggling to effectively equip the members and boost their confidence to witness.
- And if you're looking for a way to create a culture of lifestyle evangelism within your congregation.

You Are Even At An Advantaged Position In The Light Of Available Statistics When You Implement Andrew & Philip Strategy:

- A recent religious survey found that 7% of the unchurched plan to visit a church this year. Another 33 percent say they would consider returning to church. A whopping 40% of the American population is willing to attend a church event if invited by a friend.

- 21% of churchgoers invited anybody to church once a year. Interestingly only 2% of the churchgoers invited the unchurched in any given year.

What do the figures say to you and me: The church is not equipped for the most basic biblical strategy taught by Jesus? The members are not equipped to be inviters. Your church can double in one year as you implement this Andrew & Philip Strategy of "each one bring one," "one win one," and "come and see," I saw an amazing results each time this was put in place.

In fact, you just may have trouble believing the astounding numbers and the vibrant and expectant attitude that will settle on your church after implementing this lesson. A healthy dose of skepticism is good but letting it prevent you from examining a worthwhile opportunity and taking action could cost you dearly. Everything you're going to learn about is 100% true and most of the beneficiaries are still around to confirm it. I will explain why and how it works.

But First Let Me Tell You A Little More About Myself:

My name is Pastor Tommy Banks. Before Jesus Christ came into my life, I was a very different person than I am today. The joy and excitement of dramatic change in my life soon after conversion to Christ led me to soul winning. I later joined the two-evangelism team, one going out on Wednesdays and the other on Saturdays. We saw people come to Christ and some became part of the local church. I was frustrated at my soul witnessing endeavors. Many times I came before people I wanted to witness to and did not know what to say or if I knew how to say it. I knew there had to be an easier, better way to succeed in witnessing to the people. At that time I had no idea what it was because all we heard from the pulpit was "go witness and invite people to church", but never told how to do it.

So How Did I Come Up With This Evangelism & Mobilization Plan:

I was crying out for answers to the problems in my frustrations in our evangelism efforts, and I bought a book, entitle "Evangelism Explosion" by the late Dr. Kennedy. It seemed too complex to me, then a friend came back from 'Amsterdam 2007' ten-day conferences for pastors and evangelist. He brought back with him materials from Billy Graham Evangelistic Association and Campus Crusade for Christ. I knew I still needed to find some type of simplified, easy to be used by anybody, anywhere, and easily transferable plan to help us invite people to church, present Christ, and counsel the new believer. With an intense study of the Testament Bible for evangelism clues and what had been gleaned from those two great ministries this breakthrough strategy. You are reading about was developed. Thank you Holy Spirit!

Andrew & Philip Strategy:

This is simple and is the message of personal evangelism by the author and the Master Evangelist (Jesus Christ himself). We mobilize every member of the church in a prayer effort and equip him or her to effectively build bridges of friendship within the network of contacts they have. The training encourages one to use the opportunities that arise in the interaction to witness and invite the contacts to the Christian event. My program is built around and on the foundation of this strategy authored by the Master Jesus – The Andrew & Philip Strategy:

"Reach and Teach!"—"Come and See!"

Now, you're probably wondering – if this program is so great, why not use the formula to build you a church? The answer is simple. We are not all called to build a pastoral ministry. However, I am old fashioned to the extent that I believe the Holy Spirit is still in the business of appointing pastors over churches. Yes, the Holy Spirit works through people, committees, or boards, if these people allow Him. The program has been used successfully, virtually every event we had put up. This program has been tested over the last ten years and it works. In Nigeria, where today it has some of the largest and fastest growing churches, I introduce the program to a friend, and the result is in.

> Pastor Ikea, a prayer director for Reinhardt Bonkke in Africa had this to say: **"The Andrew & Philip Evangelism Strategy is unlike anything I have seen. This is absolutely the best way to learn how to witness! Its biblical approach is refreshingly straightforward, logical and most importantly, it really works!"**

Don't get me wrong. I'm not trying to get you to voluntarily commit to something you don't need, nor asking wistfully for a charitable donation. All I'm intentionally trying to do is to get you to carefully look at what is being offered. You just might agree that this is the end of your search for that workable program. A program designed to equip your members to defeat witnessing fears, attract more visitors, connect with those visitors and equip them to invite their friends. What an incredible opportunity of a typical lifetime!!!

Outlining Details of the Strategy:

My vision is to help young pastors to demonstrate in their lives and apply in their churches the biblical concepts of their role as witnesses; equipping them to reach and win the lost one person at a time. And what they do is built around the biblical strategy of "Come and See" combined with a scheduled prepared church event such as a crusade or revival.

You accomplish this vision by creating an environment and an outreach platform to practice what is taught during the training phase. In doing this, you need to provide a place for the believer and unsaved people in the community to come together to interact. A trained believer lives purposely. Such outreach platform could be a food pantry, a computer center or a church event such as a revival. My program strategy has been specially planned to help the believer build a trust relationship with those he or she comes in contact with. When the opportunity arises the believer presents Christ to the unsaved contact.

Three Stage Thrust:

The first stage of this innovative program consists of training and mobilizing the church members for prayers, and lifestyle evangelism. The hands-on training enables your church to fully engage in evangelism or crusade mobilization and the follow up to crusade event.

The follow-up: The Health and Wealth Program provide a non-threatening environment and setting for people in the community to come and participate, who may never go to the local church. When they come you educate them on health and economic matters. If they haven't heard the Gospel you share it. If they never saw the move of God you invite them to the main crusade event.

And finally, your members have an "Event" (Active Practice Environment) to use as a tool to invite friends to come and be your guests in order that they can hear a clear message of Christ's love and plan for their lives.

You Need To Design A Powerful Ministering Team:

The preaching and teaching team of your congregation should be made up of powerfully anointed people; both youths and seniors (pastors, preachers, prophets, evangelists, leaders, and laymen) with relevant experience impacting the church in the area they are called to minister. The large attendance experienced in my meetings results usually not from name recognition of the speakers but from the mobilization of the membership grassroots. You provide the speakers but should your church, or in the case of a citywide crusade, have a preference you use their speaker. The speaker must, of course, be willing to accommodate your altar call and counseling arrangement to meet the crusade (revival) objective.

Your Church Could Be A Training Center For Others:

When a church desires to see the principle at work, a crusade can be arranged using the churches premises or another designated facility for training and the subsequent crusades (revivals).

If the church is:

- Centrally located in a targeted city or community.
- Has facilities and sound equipment adequate for the expected crowd.
- Has easy access to the main highways.

Then the church is encouraged to become a base for mobilization and training for a crusade (revival) involving some of the neighboring churches. The harvest of souls, resulting from the crusade (revival) and the attendant exposure, I believe, is a fitting reward for a hosting church.

Special Worker Evangelism Seminars:

We offer every aspect of witnessing skills improvement, including ½ day, 1-day, and 2-day event training or 3-4 day seminars on request.

Why it Works All the Time:

Note! What we do (Wanda and I), we inspire and motivate people to willingly and joyfully accept and practice things unnatural in the light of prevailing influences in our world under the empowering of the Holy Spirit. It is patterned after the New Evangelism ("Reach and Teach"—"Come and See").

Will You Accept the Challenge?

It can be for you, too. I have given you all these details, so you get all the facts in order to make an informed decision. Should you decide that this is not for you, I still appreciate you taking your time to read this far; and if it's okay for you. Great!

I will be praying with you and your congregation. In addition to skill acquisition, the training days will serve as an effective means of unlocking the vision to the participants' friends and an opening door to their communities.

The key initiatives begin soon after the training. There is a multitude of alternate entry points accessible to non-believers; Crusades, Revival Meetings, Special Events, these are short term; Soup Kitchen, Computer Center, Job Readiness Program, and etc, these are long term. Different churches address spiritual needs from a distinctive perspective. You should custom tailor your training to meet your church needs. While you're working to meet the unique needs of your church, your basic format is:

1. Training.
2. Wealth and Wellness Strategies Meeting.
3. Evangelistic - Healing and Miracle Crusade (Revival).

The Key is taking a Step:

The decision isn't whether or not to believe the system works. I have proven that it does – consistently. The results speak for themselves. The questions you should be asking yourself are: Am I serious about equipping my members to overcome witnessing reluctances, acquire biblical tips on inviting people to your church events and the skill implement – The Andrew & Philip Strategy, and step out in faith and see new visitors week after week.

In the Andrew & Philip Strategy, there are Two Ways to Approach (the person to whom you are inviting and witnessing).

The first is:

1. The direct approach. This approach can be used when inviting and witnessing to:
   (a) A relative. Andrew used the direct approach to bring his brother Simon Peter to Christ (above verses 40-42).
   (b) A friend. Phillip the apostle used the direct approach to bring Nathaniel to Jesus (45-46).
   (c) The concerned. Jesus used the direct approach to win Nicodemus (John 3:1-21).
   (d) The Seeker. Paul and Silas used the direct approach to lead the Philippians' jailer to Jesus (Acts 16:19-34).

The second is:

2. The indirect approach. This approach can be used when inviting and witnessing to:

   (a) A stranger. Jesus used the indirect approach to witness to the Samaritan woman (John 4:7-26).
   (b) The religious. Phillip the evangelist used the indirect approach to lead the Ethiopian eunuch to Christ (Acts 8:26-39).

The method, in either case, will vary according to the leading of the Holy Spirit. Whether you use the direct or the indirect approach, be sure to follow through until you have presented God's Plan of Salvation and invited them to accept Jesus Christ as their personal Savior.

CHAPTER 5

WITNESSES MODEL - HOW TO WITNESS EFFECTIVELY

What Is Christian Witnessing?

(Testify to: tell what you have seen or experienced. A Christian is to be a witness by sharing a personal experience of what Jesus Christ has done in and for him or her.)

One day as Jesus walked by the Sea of Galilee he saw two men: Simon called Peter and Andrew, his brother, they were fishermen.

> "And He said unto them, Follow Me and I will make you fishers of men" (Matthew 4:19; KJV).

To be an effective witness, you must be taught, trained and motivated by the power of the Holy Spirit. Jesus took three years to teach and train His disciples in the art of soul winning. After His resurrection, He instructed them to stay in Jerusalem and "wait for the promise of the Father" (see note on Acts 1:4—8; KJV).

When you witness trust the Holy Spirit to do three things:

- Illuminate (enlighten or light up) the mind of the unbeliever. Remember all lost souls are in spiritual darkness; (see 11 Corinthians 4:3, 4).
- Prick (pierce or cut) the heart of the unbeliever. As Peter preached Christ the listeners, "Were pricked in their

hearts" (see Acts 2:37). The word "pricked" mean to penetrate or slice open.
- Change (move or encourage) the will of the unbeliever. The prodigal son returned home when he came to himself and said, "I will arise and go to my Father" (see Luke 15:18). The word "arise" tells us that the journey to God is always upward, while that with Satan is always downward.

When the disciples ask Jesus if the time had come for Him to restore the kingdom of Israel, Jesus answered,

> "It is not for you to know the times or the seasons, which the Father has put in His own power. But you shall receive power, after that the Holy Spirit is come upon you: and you shall be witnesses unto me."

On the day of Pentecost, the hundred and twenty received power to witness, and any believer who will acquire the know-how can be an effective soul winner. He can know that he and the Holy Spirit are a witnessing team.

Peter said,

> "We are His witnesses of these things; and so is also the Holy Spirit (the Spirit of Truth), whom God hath given to them that, obey Him" (Acts 5:32; KJV).

Therefore, when you witness remember,

> "Your body is the temple of the Holy Spirit (the Spirit of Truth) which is in you" (1 Cor. 6:19, 20; KJV).

You may be up-to-date in all modern techniques of soul winning, and able to quote the necessary scriptures without a flaw, but if you do not evangelize in the power of the Holy Spirit, your soul winning efforts will be ineffective.

CHAPTER 6

WITNESSES MODEL - HOW TO WITNESS PROPHETICALLY

What Is Prophetic Witnessing?

(The term "Prophetic" simply refers to witnessing and reaching out to non-believers and hurting hearts, by hearing a specific word from God to address their need for salvation, healing, and deliverance.

It is different than ordinary witnessing because it doesn't just preach the gospel but seeks to speak to the individual's life with a specific word from the Lord to them about their spiritual condition.

It is a demonstration of not only the conviction of the Word of God and the Gospel of Jesus Christ but also a display of the power of the Spirit of God to minister specifically to an individual.)

The Blood of Jesus can wash away anyone's sins. Lest there be any doubt as to whom we should witness to, God politely tells us to witness to all. As a prime example:

- A young man was dying terribly of sexual aids, because of his reckless lifestyle; even still, I went faithfully to visit him at a local hospice, to witness to him. Unbelievably, the young man humbly confessed Christ. Shortly following that he died. Someone may ask thoughtfully did this young man really get saved. Only God can satisfactorily answer that.

Jesus clearly stated,

> "All that the Father giveth me shall come to me; and him that cometh to me I will in no wise cast out"
> (John 6: 37; KJV).

This verse refers to all, whoever they are, whether Israelites, Gentiles, Pharisees, Scoffers, Harlots, or even the very Castaways of the Devil; no one has ever been turned away, and no one will ever be turned away.

We're also graciously warned according to the New Testament of First John 1:9, that God will forgive us:

> "If we confess our sins, he is faithful and just to forgive us our sins, and to cleanse us from all unrighteousness."

Note: Sin, its reality, and remedy! This verse pertains to acts of sin, whatever they might be; the sinner is to believe (John 3:16); the Saint is to confess. God will always be true to His Own Nature and Promises, keeping Faith with Himself and with the man.

"All," not some; All sin was remitted, paid for, and put away on the basis of the satisfaction offered for the demands of God's Holy Law, which sinners broke, when the Lord Jesus died on the Cross.

CHAPTER 7

WITNESSES MODEL - PROCLAMATION OF THE GOSPEL TO JESUS CHRIST

What Is Proclamation of the Gospel?

(Proclamation of the Gospel is proclaiming the gospel rightly. So people can hear the truth of salvation through the Savior, the Master, the Lord Jesus Christ, and have the opportunity to respond by faith and through repentance.)

Witnesses who are genuinely concerned for others will be looking forward to appropriate opportunities to witness to non-believers. Yes, this will be especially true as they carefully build social relationships with willing individuals and families through their evangelism ministry. Every witness will come to know personally beloved children, teenagers, and adults who are related to active church members but are not faithful Christians. God can typically use that personal relationship as a basis for the witness's natural and effective presentation of the glorious gospel. Established contact with families will also provide many unique opportunities to help Christians properly apply the everlasting gospel in their everyday lives.

Witnessing as Jesus Witnessed:

Faithful Christians naturally find Jesus to be the primary example for their proclaiming ministry. Jesus declared that preaching the kingdom of God was his primary mission (see Luke 4:43). The way he carried out that mission provides a good model for Christians to follow. Following his baptism and temptation experience, Jesus returned to Galilee where he began his ministry by teaching in the synagogues. In his hometown of Nazareth, he read from Isaiah scroll a passage that he identified with himself. Jesus knew that God's Spirit had anointed him to announce the Good News and proclaim the results of that gospel (see Luke 4:14-21).

Before the coming of Jesus, John preached as I mentioned in my previous book "Youthology," I wrote about in chapter 3, *"The preaching of John the Baptist."* And in fact, Luke the writer of the Gospel informs us in the New Testament Holy Bible, (Luke 3:3 – 6; KJV):

> "And he came into all the country about Jordan, preaching the baptism of repentance for the remission of sins: As it is written in the book of the words of Isaiah the prophet, saying, the voice of one crying in the wilderness, Prepare ye the way of the Lord, make his paths straight. Every valley shall be filled. And every mountain and hill shall be brought low; and the crooked shall be made straight, and the rough ways shall be made smooth; And all flesh shall see the salvation of God."

These Bible verses make it crystal clear that John the Baptist shouted in the wilderness. His message was "humble yourself, confess your sins and repent, receive baptism, and open the way for the Messiah to take hold of your lives." John's announcement of the Messiah's coming fell softly on no one's ears. He certainly didn't try to lead the people into believing that they could welcome the Savior with an unthinking enthusiasm like that of a child who looks forward to a new toy for Christmas.

In fact, John's message was "prepare the way of the Lord." Prepare refers to making something ready; 'way' could also be translated 'road.' Thus, part of "preparing the way" is to make His path straight.

When a king proposed to tour a part of his kingdoms in the east, he sent a messenger before him to tell the people to prepare the roads. So, John is regarded as the messenger of the King. But preparation on which he insisted was the preparation of heart and of life. He said, "The King is coming, mend, not your roads, but your life." Every one of us has the duty to make life fit for the King to see. The people of Israel, who came to see this prophet in the wilderness, were faced with a life-changing message. If they would prepare themselves—clear away the spiritual debris and straighten any crooked immoral paths—the way would be ready for their King and Messiah to come.

The Messiah that John the Baptist announced is certainly a threat to anyone who has become self-satisfied and overly comfortable with their lives, values, and opinions. The King that John called people to prepare for was the One who came to interrupt that normal course of life in order to introduce the way of God. The Christ was coming and the people needed to be prepared to meet him, even though the preparation was going to disrupt their lives.

In many marvelous ways, this naturally reminds me of an evangelical story (smile), which I'll share with you. Two young men in the glorious past carefully opened a motor vehicle detailing shop and prospered economically. Then an evangelist came to town, and one of them was saved. He tried with great enthusiasm to persuade his partner to confess his sins and accept salvation through our Lord and Savior Jesus Christ also but to no avail.

"Why won't you?" asked the born-again man.

"Listen," the other man said:

"If I confess my sins and get saved too, who's going to clean the cars?"

John the Baptist says that we have to prepare the way for Christ. If you had an important guest coming for dinner, what would you do? Whenever we have special guests coming to our house, Wanda, Tommy and I always clean up inside the house. There are so many things to do when preparing for guests—prepare a special meal, decorate with some flowers, light the good smelling candles, put on nice clothes and fix our hair, and so on. However, in my case, the significant and major preparation I do to prepare for guests is to clean certain areas of the house, especially the bathrooms, and I get rid of junk just lying around the house. In other words, cleansing the inside of your house is repentance.

What would you do if you have a very special guest coming? What is the most urgent thing you need to do to prepare for the coming Christ? Truly, we celebrate with our special guests, we enjoy one another, and we share a delicious meal. We share God's love and grace with family, friends, and neighbors. However, I believe we should, as John the Baptist proclaimed, get cleaned up inside, and recognize our sinful nature, in one word, repentance. This is the first and most urgent thing to do, in order to go to heaven.

In the scriptures, John says we need to stop and take the time to examine ourselves. Are there areas in our lives that are in need of repentance? Are there activities that we are involved in that lead others or us to unhealthy living? Are there relationships that are in need of repair or more time and attention? Do we give ourselves over to God (the Spirit of Truth) for God's purposes? John wants us to repent so that we can receive forgiveness and "see the salvation of God" (vv.6).

> "And the time of this ignorance God winked at (overlook); but now commandeth all men every where to repent (Acts 17:30)."

What is repentance? What does a person do when he or she repents? The English word 'repentance' comes from two Latin words, which means to be sorry again. Repentance is turning from sin; an act of the will whereby one resolves, by the help of God to give up his sins; a change of mind with respect to sin that leads to a change of conduct. Repentance means turning away from all sin. Some people are willing to give up all their sins except the one sin that is dearest to their hearts. Jesus said,

> "If any man will come after me, let him deny himself, and take up his cross, and follow me (Matthew 11:24)."

The word of God has much to say about repentance. All of the great preachers of both the Old and New Testaments gave repentance a central place in their messages. The prophets of Old called on the people of Israel to repent of their sins and turn to God.

When Peter preached to the multitude on the day of Pentecost, and many were converted and cried out, "Men and brethren, what shall we do? Peter said unto them, "Repent, and be baptized every one of you in the name of Jesus Christ."

Repentance is so important that God commands "all men everywhere to repent." It is a message that is greatly needed today. Men and women have forgotten God and given themselves over to sin. As they group in the darkness which has settled over the earth, and cries out, "what shall we do? If they will but listen, they will hear that call of God which came to men of old, "repent of your sins."

John spoke from the heart and mind of God, when prophetic witnessing we must be willing to take a step back and let the Holy Spirit take full control.

Meeting the Needs of our Community:

- Uniting Together:
    1. Union with God and other Christians; those who are joined with the Lord are one spirit with Him. True followers bring forth fruit.

- Promoting Outreach:
    1. To the Broken Hearts.
    2. To the Hungry and Poor.
    3. To the Un'churched; nonbelievers introduce them to a living relationship with Jesus Christ. In the Bible, (Ephesians 4:15; KJV) tells us to, *"Speak the Truth in Love."*

- Showing Consistency:
    1. Faithfulness.
    2. Along with faithfulness, we need wisdom; wisdom to understand the time and contexts into which Christ has called us to serve as His witnesses.

WITNESSES MODEL PROCLAMATION OF THE GOSPEL

As we scroll through our communities, we need to look carefully at the neighborhoods we are in; we live in a notoriously violent society. Lots of people are heartbroken, abused, used and bruised by circumstances, poor relationships with others, sinfulness, and physical testing. Throughout His ministry on earth, Jesus met people in desperate need of help. Bible verses (Mark 1:1 - 2) tell us,

> "The beginning of the gospel of Jesus Christ, the Son of God; as it is written in the prophets, Behold, I send my messenger before thy face, which shall prepare thy way before thee."

In this verse, Mark starts his narrative with a simple declaration of the Good News about God's Son, the Lord Jesus Christ. As Luke notes in Bible verse Acts 1 and 1, the Gospel stories describe what "Jesus began both to do and teach." The gospel refers to the basic story of the Good News to be found in Christ's life, ministry, death, and resurrection. "Jesus", meaning "Yahweh saves," is the earthly name Jesus received at birth, whereas "Christ" is an Old Testament title that designates Him as God's chosen servant. The phrase "Son of God" makes clear Jesus' deity and demonstrates His unique relationship with God, His father. In this quotation from "as it is written in the prophets," proclaims the Old Testament as the Word of God; John the Baptist and the writer Mark proclaims the coming of the King of all Kings, Jesus Christ. You see, in ancient times, a messenger was sent ahead to announce the coming of the king. Local communities would often repair rough roads to ensure the comfort of the king as he traveled.

Perhaps as you are confronted with the person of Jesus Christ in this study, you will be compelled to witness of these things, by the unction (see 1 John 2:20) of "the Holy Ghost, whom God hath given to them that obey Him" (see Acts 5:32), to tell others about Jesus; as per say the Samaritan woman had done. She let the cat out of the bag, according to the Holy Bible, (John 4, 28 – 29):

> "The woman then left her water pot, and went her way
> into the city, and saith to the men, come, see a man,
> which told me all things that I did: is not this the Christ?"

In her excitement, the women exaggerated. She did not report what Jesus actually told her, but what He could have told her. Note the woman's spiritual journey. She first viewed Christ as a Jew (verse 9), then as a prophet (verse 19), and finally as the Messiah. Her question presupposes that, as stated, her fellow Samaritans were looking for a Messiah.

You must be willing to help meet the needs of the broken and hungry hearts in your community. The question is; are you willing to help those who are in need of help? If your response is yes! Please begin by opening your eyes and carefully observing the people around you, so that you can learn to say more effectively the witnessing of the Gospel that lives in your heart.

Sharing Good News with Lost Souls:

As the opportunity arises you need to tell people how you got saved, give them a chance to do the same, and trust the Holy Spirit to do the rest. What an excitement and thrill it is to be able to share the Gospel message with others. Winning souls for Christ is never in vain! In the Old Testament, Proverbs 11:30 naturally tells us that precious, "The fruit of the righteous is a tree of life and he that wins souls is wise." Therefore, he who tells others about Jesus is; in effect, presenting to them "a tree of life." This simply means that it is wise to win dear souls to Jesus! Soul winning is sharing the Gospel of Jesus Christ with lost sinners, is an effort to WIN them to Christ.

As I conclude with the life of Christ throughout our present-day society, I can honestly say that when we come to the Christ of the Gospels we are at the basis of the New Testament and the fulfillment of much of the Old. Even better put are the inspired words of the apostle Paul who wrote,

> "For by him were all things created, that are in heaven,
> and that are in earth, visible and invisible, whether they

> be thrones, or dominions, or principalities, or powers:
> all things were created by him. And for him: And
> he is before all things, and by him all things consist"
> (Colossian 1:16, and 17; KJV).

I thank God, Jesus Christ is not only the moral standard of eternal righteousness, but He's also the source of it. He is both the pattern and the provision for the Christian walk. It was the death of Christ which saved us from sin in the past; it is the life of Christ which delivers us from sin in the present and future. Paul wrote in (Romans 5:9 - 10) which articulates,

> "Much more then, being now justified by his blood, we
> shall be saved from wrath through him. For if, when we
> were enemies, we were reconciled to God by the death of
> his Son, much more, being reconciled, we shall be saved
> by his life."

Again in Romans chapter 6, we are told as Christians we died to sin when we identified with Christ in faith (verses 1-4); thus, we have been freed from the dominion of sin to live a life of obedience to God (verses 5-11). This new beginning should become a continuing reality in our lives.

Conversion Cycle of the Past:

- Person (come and see)
- Church (next step)
- Salvation
- God

In the Old Testament God dwelt in the tabernacle, and nonbelievers was drawn to the church for answers and evangelism. The church is the primary path to salvation, fellowship, and a healthy growing relationship with God by showing a willingness to obey.

The New Cycle:

- Person (reach and teach — come and see)
- Salvation (next step)
- Church
- God

In the New Testament, God dwells in our human body; He becomes us and we become him. We are a royal priesthood that functions in a ruling capacity, like kings. Because we are borne with a price; in the Bible, **(First Corinthians 6:20)**, **"For ye are bought with a price: therefore glorify God in your body, and in your spirit, which are God's."**

What this means in more detail is that we belong to God because He created us into a house of His Spirit. And He has purchased us with the shed blood of His Son, Jesus Christ at Calvary.

Therefore, since few nonbelievers today go to church or church-sponsored events for answers, evangelism must often take place as an encounter outside the church building. The church role is to prepare Christians for these encounters and provide safe entry points for new believers to enter into true church life. We are to reach those in darkness and bring them to the light.

Ask yourself, have you done all you canned to help the church or un-churched (see First Corinthians 11:31) and does it bring divine glory to God? If God is going to hold us accountable for every idle word spoken, then you can count on it that He will reward us for even the most seemingly insignificant acts of faith.

CHAPTER 8

WITNESSES MODEL - HOW TO SHARE GOD'S PLAN OF SALVATION

What Is God's Plan of Salvation?

(God's Plan of Salvation comes only by God's grace and through His Son when a person accepts Jesus Christ as Lord and Savior.)

"For God so loved the world that he gave his only begotten Son, that whosoever believeth in him should not perish, but have everlasting life" (John 3:16; KJV).

There are seven simple steps to take in sharing God's Plan of Salvation.

1. Share your personal experience of salvation. Don't give your life story. It should not take more than a few minutes to tell how the Lord saved you. As you come to the close of your testimony, bring out your Bible and say, may I share with you God's plan of salvation that change my life?
2. Now read (John 3:16) on the love of God. When you come to the close of the reading say something like this: Tom (or Sue) will you now admit that God loves you. Lead him (or her) to admit it if you can. This will get him (or her) involved in the plan of salvation.
3. Now read (Romans 3:23-26), "**For all have sinned, and come short of the glory of God; Being justified**

freely by his grace through the redemption that is in Christ Jesus: Whom God hath set forth to be a propitiation through faith in his blood, to declare his righteousness for the remission of sins that are past, through the forbearance of God; To declare, I say, at this time his righteousness: that he might be just, and the justifier of him which believeth in Jesus."

After reading the scripture, ask him (or her) to admit that he (or she) is a lost sinner. When he (or she) admits that he (or she) is a lost sinner, you say something like this: Tom (or Sue), isn't it wonderful, God loves you even though you are a lost sinner.

4. Now, you have already confessed and admitted that you are a sinner. Now, God would have you know that "the wages of sin is death." You are dead in sin until you accept Jesus Christ as personal Saviour. The Apostle Paul said, "**You hath he quickened, who were dead in trespasses and sins**" (Ephesians 2:1). To be saved is to be made spiritually alive in Jesus Christ.

   What is death?

   1) Death is spiritual separation. Your sins have separated you from God; you are dead in your sins.
   2) Death is physical separation; it separates the spirit and soul from the body.
   3) Death is eternal separation. If you remain lost in your sins, you will stand before God at the great white throne judgment, and there your sins will separate you from the mercy of God forever; this is hell (see notes on Revelation 20:11-15).

   You know that God loves you, and that you are a sinner—dead in sins. Admit to yourself: "I am dead in sins." When he (or she) admits that he (or she) is dead in sin, say something like this: Tom (or Sue) isn't it great, even though you are a lost sinner dead in sin, God loves you.

5. Now read (Romans 5:6), "**For when we were yet without strength, in due time Christ died for the ungodly.**" He died for those who are unlike God; this includes you. "**While we were yet sinners, Christ died for us**" (verse 8).

"**For he (God the Father) hath made him (God the Son) to be made sin for us, who knew no sin; that we might be made the righteousness of God in him**" (11 Corinthians 5:21).

"**For as much as ye know that ye were not redeemed with corruptible things, as silver and gold, from your vain conversation received by tradition from your fathers; But with the precious blood of Christ, as of a lamb without blemish and without spot**" (1 Peter 1:18-19).

"**For Christ also hath once suffered for sin, the just for the unjust, that he might bring us to God, being put to death in the flesh, but quickened by the spirit**" (1 Peter 3:18).

"**Christ died for our sins according to the scriptures**" (1 Corinthians 15:3).

In the light of these wonderful Scriptures, will you now thank God for His great love in sending His Son to bear your sins in His own body on the cross, and admit to yourself that: "Christ died on Calvary for me." Say something like this: Tom (or Sue) isn't it wonderful, isn't it great that God loves you so much that He died on Calvary bearing your sins.

6. Now share with him/her (Acts 16:30-31), "**And brought them out, and said, Sir, what must I do to be saved? And they said, Believe on the Lord Jesus Christ, and thou shalt be saved, and thy house.**"

The Philippian jailer asked Paul and Silas: "Sir, what must I do to be saved?" the answer was quick in response, and positive in content: "Believe on the Lord Jesus Christ, and thou shalt be saved, and thy house. Paul and Silas preached the gospel to the jailer and those in his house; they believed and were saved. (Note: As we continue, some references are made as direct statements to an unsaved person, some to the faithful Christian. Let your heart judge which you are.)

What is this gospel that saves when believed? It is:

First, "That Christ died for our sins."

Second, "That he was buried."

Third, "That he rose again the third day" (Typically see First Corinthians 15:3, 4).

Jesus Christ the God-man died for you, was buried for you, and rose from the dead for you; and is now at the right hand of the Father interceding for you (see 1 John 2:1).

"For I am not ashamed of the gospel of Christ; for it is the power of God unto salvation to everyone that believeth" (see Romans 1:16). The gospel is the power of God unto salvation only when you believe. Your faith in Jesus Christ releases the power of God that saves your soul.

The man born blind received physical sight by a miracle, but spiritual sight came when Jesus asked, "Dost thou believe on the Son of God?" he answered, "Lord, I believe" (see John 9:35-38). Salvation came to Thomas when he believed, and confessed, "My Lord and my God" (see John 20:24-29).

When you confess with your mouth the Lord Jesus, and believe in your heart that God hath raised Him from the dead, you will be saved (see Romans 10:9, 10).

Accept him (or her) now by faith, and pray this prayer: "Lord Jesus, I know you died on the cross bearing my sins. Thank you, Lord, for revealing to me my lost, sinful condition. I confess that I am a sinner, dead in sin, and cannot save myself. I do now by faith, gladly accept you as my personal Saviour, and thank you, Lord, for eternal salvation. Amen."

7. Now lead him/her to call upon the name of the Lord in prayer, "**For whosoever shall call upon the name of the Lord shall be saved.**"

In the Bible (Acts 4:12) says,

> "Neither is there salvation in any other: for there is none other name under heaven given among men, whereby we must be saved."

This proclaims without a doubt that Jesus alone holds the plan to Salvation and in fact is Salvation. This says it all. It begins on earth and finds completion at death or at Christ's return.
In the well-worn Bible (Titus 2:11-14) articulates,

> "For the grace of God that bringeth salvation hath appeared to all men; teaching us that, denying ungodliness and worldly lust, we should live soberly, righteously, and godly, in this present world; looking for that blessed hope, and the glorious appearing of the great God and our Saviour Jesus Christ; who gave himself for us, that he might redeem us from all iniquity, and peculiar people, zealous of good works."

Note: On the Cross, Christ died for every sin; past, present and future, at least for all who will believe (John 3:16). There are three vital means for one to receive the gift of salvation: One must hear, repent and believe.

1. One Must Hear: Hearing is the avenue to faith. Because the Bible scripture (Hebrews 11:6) tell us that, "**Without faith it is impossible to please God**;" (Romans 10:17) says, "**So then faith cometh by hearing and hearing by the word of God**;" and Jesus said according to (Matthew 11:15), "**He that hath ears to hear, let him hear.**"
2. One Must Repent: Repent means to turn or change to God's way of living; repentance is one of the first means to becoming a Christian. In the Gospel according to (Mark 1:15) Jesus said, "**The time is fulfilled, and the kingdom of God is at hand: repent ye, and believe the gospel.**" The gospel refers to the basic story of the Good News to be found in Christ's life, ministry, death, and resurrection.
3. One Must Believe: Believe means to trust in God with commitment, obedience, and faith. It is a commitment of both mind and heart. In the Bible (verse 16 c,) of the Gospel according to John, chapter 3 says, "**That whosoever believeth in him should not perish, but have everlasting life.**" Salvation is the divine act of God, which delivers the spirit, heart and soul of a person from the chains of sin, slavery, death and hell. It is forgiveness of sin. Being born again of the word of God and made a citizen of God's kingdom on earth. Salvation is also a fruit of the Holy Spirit, off the tree of life in the midst of the Paradise of God.

In the Word of God (Romans 10:9-10) says,

"If thou shalt confess with thy mouth the Lord Jesus,
and shalt believe in thine heart that God hath raised him
from the dead, thou shalt be saved. For with the heart

man believeth unto righteousness; and with the mouth
confession is made unto salvation."

You see, when faith comes forth from its silence to announce itself and proclaim the Glory and the Grace of the Lord, its voice is confession.

Please, consider (Romans 6:23),

"For the wages of sin is death, but the gift of God is
eternal life through Jesus Christ our Lord."

This well-known Bible verse is often used when presenting the Gospel. To show that unsaved sinners will pay for their "SIN" with eternal separation from God. Throughout death and that they can escape that death through the gift of eternal life that Jesus Christ provides.

There's nothing we can do to earn our salvation. God's Holy Word tells us according to (Ephesians 2:8-9),

"For by grace are ye saved through faith; and that not of
yourselves: it is the gift of God: Not of works, lest any
man should boast."

We find that the grace of God is the source of our salvation. Our faith is the channel and not the cause. God alone saves.

CHAPTER 9

WITNESSES MODEL - HOW TO GIVE THE INVITATION

What Is the Invitation About?

(It's about the passionate cry of the Holy Spirit to a hurting, lost, and dying world. And what Jesus willingly did for all on the illuminated cross and therefore, all can be miraculously saved, if they will only just come to Him.

Kindly invite the person {to whom you are witnessing} to by faith voluntarily accept the Lord Jesus Christ as his or her personal Savior.)

"And the Spirit and the bride say Come. And let him that heareth say, Come. And let him that is athirst come. And whosoever will, let him take the water of life freely" (Revelation 22:17; KJV).

As I have said beforehand in chapters 1 and 4 (The Philippian jailer, equally known as the earnest seeker had to graciously hear to sincerely believe {typically see Acts 16:19-40}). And now, I say again, the Philippian jailer asked Paul and Silas:

"Dear Sir, what must I do to be saved?" the straightforward answer was positive and quick in response:

"Believe on the Lord Jesus Christ, and thou shalt be saved, and thy house. Paul and Silas preached the gospel to the prison guard and those in his house; they sincerely believed and were saved."

(Note: As we continue thoughtfully, some references are made as direct statements to an unsaved person, some to the faithful Christian. Willingly let your heart judge which you are incomparable.)

Then you say gently something like this: Tom (or Sue), will you bow your head with me in prayer as I humbly ask the dear Lord to miraculously save you, right here and now?"

Don't wait for him (or her) to bow his (or her) head. You lead the way. If he (or she) will not bow with you, don't force it. Pray a short prayer that the Lord will convict him (or her) of sin and bring him (or her) to repentance. Lift up your head and make an appointment to return for another witness session. If he (or she) does not pray with you, pray a brief, silent prayer. Ask the Lord to save him (or her) now.

Now, ask him to pray after you the prayer of acceptance:

"Lord Jesus, I know you died on the cross bearing my sins. Thank you, Lord, for revealing to me my lost, sinful condition. I confess that I am a sinner, dead in sin, and cannot save myself. I do now by faith, gladly accept you as my personal Saviour, and thank you, Lord, for eternal salvation. Amen."

You pray, "Lord Jesus, I know you love me." Now he (or she) prays, "Lord Jesus, I know you love me." Continue in this manner until you have lead him (or her) through the prayer.

Now, when you have finished leading him (or her) through the prayer lift up your head and say, Tom (or Sue), did you by faith accept the Lord Jesus Christ as your personal Savior as you prayed: 'I DO NOW BY FAITH, GLADLY ACCEPT YOU AS MY PERSONAL SAVIOR, AND THANK YOU LORD, FOR ETERNAL SALVATION. AMEN. When he (or she) answers yes, take him (or her) by the hand and say, "UPON THE AUTHORITY OF GOD'S WORD YOU ARE NOW A CHILD OF GOD."

Then read victorious Romans 10:13, it boldly says, "**For whosoever shall call upon the name of the Lord shall be saved.**" This properly speaks of the chief sinner naturally coming to Christ (anyone, anywhere), but can equally refer to any believer and with whatever need; Jesus Christ remains the effective means by which he faithfully performs all of this.

INVITATION: **If you would like to talk to someone about Jesus Christ, or you would like prayer, contact <u>gow3fold@aol.com</u>**

CHAPTER 10

WITNESSES MODEL - HOW TO FOLLOW UP

What Is the Meaning of Following Up?

(When you have properly led a precious soul to Christ, your independent responsibility does not end. You have a spiritual baby, and that baby needs help if it is to grow properly in the divine grace and eternal knowledge of the Lord Jesus Christ.)

"And they continued steadfastly in the apostles' doctrine and fellowship, and in breaking of bread, and in prayers" (Acts 2:42; KJV).

There are seven remarkable things that you can do that will willingly help the new Christian to grow spiritually.

1. Give him (or her) The Holy Bible if he (or she) does not already have one.
2. Explain God's Words (Holy Bible) and how it works.
3. Now show him (or her) how he (or she) can know that he (or she) is saved (a born-again believer).
4. To start him (or her) outright, stress the fact that we are to obey the Lord in all things.
5. Lead him (or her) into a New Testament Church (with fellow born-again believers). Say something like this: "Tom (or Sue), I am a member of a New Testament church, and I want you to be my guest at the next service." Take him

(or her) to church (fellow born-again believers), sit with him (or her), and when the invitation is given, ask him (or her) to go forward with you to make his (or her) public profession of faith in Christ (see Matthew 10:32).
6. Encourage him (or her) to witness, "**Let redeemed of the Lord say so, whom he hath redeemed from the hand of the enemy; and gathered them out of the lands, from the east, and from the west, from the north, and from the south**" (Palmas 107:2 - 3).
7. Now help him (or her) through the study of God's Words from the Holy Bible New Testament. When you have reached a certain study cycle, he (or she) should be in the church (fellow born-again believers), with a doctrinal foundation on which to continue to grow spiritually. And by now he (or she) should be involved in evangelism. He (or she) is ready to go with the Gospel.

CHAPTER 11

WITNESSES MODEL - HOW DO I KNOW I'M SAVED

Can You Be Saved and Know It?

(Yes, every "born again" child of God has the threefold proof of being saved—proof that he or she is a child of God.)

"<u>Whosoever believeth that Jesus is the Christ is born of God</u>: and every one that loveth him that begat loveth him also that is begotten of him" (1 John 5:1; KJV).

This threefold proof is: first, inward proof; second, outgoing proof; and third, outward proof.

1. "Whosoever believeth that Jesus is the Christ is born of God" (above verse 1). My faith in Christ—that He is God—is personal evidence that I am a child of God (below verses 10, 13). This is inward proof of being saved.
2. "Everyone that loveth is born of God" (see notes on 1 John 4:7-11). We are to love our fellow man with the love of God. This we are not capable of doing in the flesh; we must let God love man through us (see Romans 5:5). This is outgoing proof of being saved.
3. "Every one that doeth righteousness is born of him" (see 1 John 2:29). If you are born of God, you will make a practice of doing right at all times and at all cost (see 11 Corinthians 5:17). This is outward proof of being saved.

If you do not have the threefold proof of eternal life, now is the time to bow your head, pray, and accept Jesus Christ as your personal Saviour—by faith in His vicarious death, burial and resurrection.

Yes, It Is a Fact That You Can Be Saved and Know It

In the Bible, it says:

"<u>He that believeth on the Son of God hath the witness in himself</u>: he that believeth not God hath made him a liar; because he believeth not the record that God gave of his Son."

"These things have I written unto you that believe on the name of the Son of God; <u>that ye may know that ye have eternal life, and that ye may believe on the name of the Son of God</u>" (1 John 5:10, 13; KJV).

The Knowledge of Eternal Life

Upon the authority of God's Word, you can be saved and know it. Your faith in God's infallible Word is your assurance of salvation. "He that believeth on the Son hath (present tense) everlasting life (see John 3:36).

The Bible is a book of certainties. It strengthens convictions, and establishes beliefs. God would have you know:

1. That you are now a child of God (see 1 John 3:36).
2. That you have been made the righteousness of God in Christ (11 Corinthians 5:21).
3. That you are now a new creature in Christ (11 Corinthians 5:17).
4. That you are now a son and heir of God (Galatians 4:7).

Could you have greater assurance than is found in God's infallible Word? "Heaven and earth shall pass away, but my words shall not pass away" (see Matthew 24:35).

God Saved You to Obey Him

> "Then Peter and the other apostles answered
> and said, <u>we ought to obey God rather than men</u>"
> (Acts 5:29; KJV).

You now belong to Jesus Christ. He is your Lord and Master, Jesus Christ, in all things:

1. Unite with a New Testament church (fellow born-again believers). "And the Lord added to the church (fellow born-again believers) daily such as should be saved" (Acts 2:47).
2. Follow Him in the ordinance of baptism (see Acts 2:41).
3. Join a Sunday-school (Bible-class) and study the Word with God's children (see 11 Timothy 2:15).
4. Attend the worship services of your church (with fellow born-again believers).

In the New Testament Bible, Hebrews 10:25:

> "<u>Not forsaking the assembling of ourselves together</u>, as
> the manner of some is; but exhorting one another: and so
> much the more, as ye see the day approaching."

In this short rich passage right at the beginning of this paragraph, let's carefully notice that the emphasis is not upon attending a church building where organized religion is practiced; but rather, upon assembling with fellow born-again believers. Can I be honest with you? Today, most of the people who attend church Sunday after Sunday have never obeyed Hebrews 10:25, because they are not saved themselves, nor are they meeting with fellow born-again believers.

For example, in some of these places, it's all about religion—without any truth of God's Word. They are the blind leading the blind. As a result, I call it 'a prison house of religion.'

In fact, Jesus speaks in Matthew 16:18:

> "And I say also unto thee, that thou art Peter, <u>and upon this rock I will build my church</u>; and the gates of hell shall not prevail against it."

For instance, Jesus did not say that he would build his church upon Peter, but upon Himself, the Rock of Ages.

Again, notice the underline wording in the above verse 18, "<u>And upon this rock I will build my church</u>." Now, therefore, let us notice what the meaning of the term "rock" is. For example: "It is the revelation of truth." The Lord changed his name from Simon to Peter, which means "a little rock (a fragment of a stone)." Jesus Christ Himself is the Big Rock (the Living Stone, and the chief Corner Stone) on which the Redeemed as little living stones are built; for other foundation can no man lay than that is laid, which is Jesus Christ (see 1 Corinthians 3:11).

Therefore the writer of Hebrews 10:25, clearly instructs all born-again believers not to follow the example of those who forsake the assembly. True, "forsake" means to abandon or desert, leave, leave high and dry, turn ones back on, cast aside:

A person who believes he or she is a Christian (a follower of Jesus Christ) should in fact be present for every opportunity to worship with fellow born-again believers. It is the Lord's Time, and those who claim to belong to the Lord have appointments to keep!

1. Be a faithful steward (see 1 Corinthians 4:2). All that you are and have belong to God. "Ye are not your own. For you are bought with a price (1 Corinthians 6:19, 20). As a faithful steward, you will bring God His tithe (see Malachi 3:10 Old Testament). The tithe is one-tenth of your income, and it is the Lord's (see Leviticus 27:30 Old Testament).
2. Make time in your daily life to pray and read God's Word that you may grow in the grace and knowledge of the Lord Jesus Christ.

CHAPTER 12

WITNESSES MODEL - HOW TO LIVE DAILY WITH GOD AFTER YOU GET SAVED

So how do we learn properly to do God's will? To Abide in Him, Every Single Day, after we get saved from Sin?

> *(When we read diligently or graciously hear His eternal Word; the well-worn Holy Bible and the Scriptures. He speaks naturally to us. When we humbly pray, we speak sincerely to Him. And when we worship Him and faithfully obey Him, we are doing His will and willingly participating in His work.)*
>
> "*Love not the world, neither the things that are in the world. If any man loves the world, the love of the Father is not in him.* For all that is in the world, the lust of the flesh, and the lust of the eyes, and the pride of life, is not of the Father, but is of the world. *And the world passeth away, and the lust thereof: but he that doeth the will of God abideth forever.*"
> (1 John 2:15, 16, 17; KJV).

When we come willingly to our Lord Jesus Christ, the shattered walls between us and God are torn down. And the very presence of God, Himself, came to live in your faithful heart and my faithful heart through his Holy Spirit. As a direct result, we now know God and He instantly knows us. Think about it: We heartily have a personal relationship with the God of the eternal universe!

But like any other relationship, it dearly needs to be sincerely nurtured and naturally strengthened. If it isn't, it will wither and grow cold; God will seem distant to us, and we will no longer think of Him as our faithful friend. We might even drift into shameful behaviors that don't honor Him and instead lead us to terrible destruction. The Bible warns, **"Love not the world, neither the things that are in the world."** (The "world" spoken of here by John pertains to the ordered system of which Satan is the head).

"If we love the world, we do not have the love of the Father in us." (You see, God the Father will not share the love that must go exclusively from Him with the world).

"For all that is in the world (there is nothing in the system of this world that is of God)**: the lust of the flesh** (refers to evil cravings, wanting to please our sinful selves)**, and the lust of the eyes** (craves, wanting the sinful things we see)**, and the pride of life** (that which trust its own power and resources, and shamefully despises and violates Divine Laws and human rights)**, is not of the Father, but is of the world."** (These things have the system of the world as their source, not the Heavenly Father).

"And the world passeth away and the lust thereof (all the things that people want, whatever the allurements of the world (i.e. charm, attractiveness, seductiveness), they will soon fade away)**: but he that doeth the will of God abideth forever** (the one who keeps on habitually doing the Will of God; in other words, whoever does what God wants will live forever)**."**

If Jesus Christ is not strictly the object of our faith, God looks at everything else as worldliness. No matter how religious our efforts may be otherwise, it is still looked at by God as friendship with the world. This means the person in essence becomes an enemy of God.

Don't Follow the Enemies of God

"You adulterers and adulteresses, know ye not that the friendship of the world is enmity with God? <u>Whosoever therefore will be a friend of the world is the enemy of God</u>" (James 4:4; KJV).

My dear friend, we are to look exclusively to the Son and the Father regarding all our needs; to look elsewhere, or rather for one's faith to be placed in that other than God, presents the person as committing spiritual adultery.

Needless to say, the end is near! We have heard that the enemy of God is coming. And now many enemies of God are already here. So we know that the end is near.

These enemies love the things of the world. So whoever chooses to be a friend of the world makes himself an enemy of God. Allow me to once again make the statement that if your aim is to enjoy the evil pleasure of the world, you cannot also be a friend of God.

So let the words of God therefore abide in you, which you have read from the Holy Bible. If you do that, you will always be abiding in the Son and in the Father. And this is what God promised you—eternal life. So continue to live daily with God, as the Holy Spirit directs you.

Yes, my dear friend, live daily with Him. If you do this, you can be without fear on the day when Jesus Christ comes again. You will not need to hide and be ashamed when He comes.

You know that God always did what was right. So you know that all those who do what is right are God's children.

God has loved us so much! This shows how much He loved us: As a result of His love to us, there are six things that happen when we live daily with God after we get saved.

1. <u>We become a child of God</u>. As John 1:12-13 says, "**But as many as received him, to them gave he power to become the sons of God, even to them that believe on his name: Which were born, not of blood, nor of the will of the flesh, nor of the will of man, but of God.**" (For example, some did not accept Jesus; nevertheless, some did receive Him, and some do receive Him, "**to them He gave power to become the sons of God**," this constitutes one of the greatest promises in the Word of God, "**even to them that believe on his name**; in short, what this means is that, to have faith in Christ and

in what He has done for us at the Cross alone can make a person a son or daughter of God").

"**Which were born, not of blood** (this means that men become God's children not by natural birth)**, nor of the will of the flesh** (you see, man cannot earn Salvation, it is a free gift, received when a person accepts Jesus Christ as Lord and Savior)**, nor of the will of man** (this refers to man's religious efforts, it is not by human power or agency that we become children of the Most High)**, but of God**." (Nevertheless, God produces the change, and Salvation is not at all of man, but altogether of God.

The heart is change by His power. No unaided effort of man, no work of ours, can produce this change. At the same time, it is true that no man is renewed who does not himself desire to be a believer; for the effect of the change is on his will, and no one is changed who does not strive to enter in at the strait gate (see Philippians 2:12, 13).

These important verses, therefore, teaches us:

1. That if we are saved we must be born again.
2. That this work is the work of God; no man can do it for us.
3. That our salvation is not the result of our birth, or any honorable or pious parentage.
4. That the children of the rich and the noble, as well as the poor, must be born of God if they will be saved.
5. That the children of religious parents must be born again; or they cannot be saved. None will go to heaven simply because their parents are Christians.
6. That we should forsake all human dependence, cast off all confidence in the flesh, and go at once to the throne of grace, and ask God to adopt us into his family and save our souls from death).

2. <u>We become an heir of God</u>. In Ephesians 2:19, Paul speaks of the present state of all believers, "**Now therefore ye are no more strangers and foreigners, but fellow citizens with the saints, and of the household of God.**" (This verse tells us that the Gentiles are no more of what they once were, but speaks of them (non-Jewish people, meaning us) now having access the same as Jews, all due to what Christ did for them (us) on the cross. We belong to God's family).
3. <u>We become a new creature</u>; miraculously saved by the precious blood; a new creation. In Second Corinthians 5:17, "**Therefore if any man be in Christ, he is a new creature: behold, all things are become new.**" (You instantly see the dear old is no longer useable, with everything willingly given to us now by Christ as new).
4. <u>We become a willing servant of God</u>. In Deuteronomy 10:12-13, Moses says enthusiastically, "**And now, Israel, what doth the Lord thy God require of thee, but to fear the Lord thy God, to walk in all his ways, and to love him, and to serve the Lord thy God with all thy heart and with all thy soul, To keep the commandments of the Lord, and his statutes, which I command thee this day for thy good?**" (God had abundantly shown great favor to Israel. What in return did He typically require? Only that they would justly fear Him, sincerely love Him, and faithfully obey Him. We as well are to fear Him, love Him, and obey Him).
5. <u>We become a priest of God</u>. In Revelation 1:6, the apostle John says, "**And hath made us kings and priests unto God and his Father; to him be glory and dominion forever and ever. Amen.**" (This is made possible by God's love for us, and only by God's love for us. "God so loved us that he gave his only begotten Son, that whosoever believeth in him should not perish, but have everlasting life" (see John 3:16). Christ is the Redeemer, so He deserves the "Glory and Dominion," which will be His forever and ever.) Therefore we should consider the

facts testifying to the apostle Peter, in First Peter 2:9-10, which says, "**But ye are a chosen generation, a royal priesthood, an holy nation, a peculiar people; that ye should show forth the praises of him who hath called you out of darkness into his marvelous light; Which in time past were not a people, but are now the people of God: which had not obtained mercy, but now have obtained mercy.**" (Each person (talking earnestly about the Saints) is God's unique possession, just as if that person were the only human being in existence. Without God, there is no standing in any capacity, but we are the people of God. This is made possible by God. You see, Mercy is a product of Grace, which is a product of Jesus Christ our living Redeemer).

6. <u>We get Heavenly citizenship</u>. In Philippians 3:20-21, Paul says humbly, "**But there's far more to life for us. We're citizens** (resident) **of high heaven! We're waiting the arrival of the Saviour, the Lord Jesus Christ, who will transform our earthy bodies into glorious bodies like his own. He'll make us beautiful and whole with the same powerful skill by which he is putting everything as it should be, under and around him** (The Message Bible)." (Typically meaning the other ways will have no place in Heaven; every saintly person will have a glorified body. All eternal things are done precisely through the Savior, the divine Master, the Lord Jesus Christ, as God Himself through His Holy Spirit).

These triumphantly conclude the six remarkable things that happen naturally when we live every day with God after we get saved. If you review these lessons over and over again, you will continue growing in the knowledge of our dear Lord and divine Saviour Jesus Christ. To wisely conclude your study of the Witnesses Model - Proclamation of the Gospel, turn to the pages following this outstanding chapter. Over here you will find the Witness Model – Official Conclusion on the Witness Model – Proclamation of the Gospel inspirational book. It is humbly suggested that to get the most out of these philosophical studies, you faithfully follow them in the order given. And take time to read carefully each Scripture reference found in the explanatory notes. It is my earnest prayer that these valuable lessons will willingly help to properly establish you in genuine faith and give you spiritual confidence to evangelize, to GO WITH THE GOSPEL.

CHAPTER 13

WITNESSES MODEL – OFFICIAL CONCLUSION

God has willingly given faithful pastors, presiding bishops, the chosen apostles, inspired prophets, famed and nameless evangelists, deacons, active missionaries, inspirational leaders, and prominent laymen great responsibility through the Great Commission. But he also gives us tremendous help to realistically accomplish this responsible task. He has voluntarily committed himself through the person of the Holy Spirit *(the Comforter, the Spirit of Truth; willingly see John 16:7-15)* to come along sides us and undoubtedly helps us evangelize the corrupt world.

Sincere Christians naturally want to be obedient to the dear Lord. They earnestly desire to instantly reach the lost. But many fear or may have a moral sense of being overwhelmed at the task of global evangelism. It is true that this specific task is great. But fear and apparent hopelessness are properly removed as the church typically gets a better grip on the Holy Spirit's leading role in evangelism.

It helps tremendously to gratefully remember that the Almighty God comes alongside us. And willingly help us faithfully fulfill our divine mandate to properly equip our active members to be inviters and witnesses — the goal of the eternal process.

I have come to properly understand that what witnesses do is found in the very name itself 'witness.' Faithful witnesses are to abundantly testify: politely tell what they have naturally seen or experienced. A Christian is to be a witness by sharing personal experience of what Jesus Christ has done in and for him (or her). They are to be spiritual helpers working alongside their pastor. As partners with the pastor, witnesses have the privilege and opportunity to share in modeling ministry to the church.

Another part of what witnesses do is to proclaim the gospel to both nonbelievers and believers. Witnesses who are concerned for others will be sensitive to appropriate opportunities to witness to non-Christians. This will be especially true as they build relationships with individuals and families through their mission ministry. God can use those personal relationships as a basis for witnesses giving a natural presentation of the gospel. Sometimes God will empower or lead one to speak out to challenge community attitudes, morels, and actions with biblical principles. Witnesses need to be examples to the church and community in proclaiming the Message of God. I am convinced that the believer role of witnessing as expressed in the New Testament is appropriate today. We must honor each opportunity as a moment created and planned by Christ and what He did for us at the Cross. **"So we are ambassadors for Christ, as though God were making His appeal through us; we (as Christ's representatives) plead with you on behalf of Christ to be reconciled to God"** (see 2 Corinthians 5:20; AMP).

ENDNOTES

1. Scripture quotations marked KJV are taken from the Holy Bible, King James Version, copyright © 1975 by Thomas Nelson Inc., Publishers Nashville, Tennessee. All right reserved.
2. Scripture quotations marked MSG are taken from The Message: The Bible in Contemporary English, copyright © 1993, 1994, 1995, 1996, 2000, 2001, and 2002. Used by permission of NavPress Publishing Group.
3. From both of my books: Youthology- defining yourself, copyright © 2010 by Tommy R. Banks, Sr., ISBN 9781615798803.
4. Dangerous Crossing- Look, Listen, and Live, copyright © 2013 by Tommy R. Banks, Sr. Registration Number TX 7-911-343 May 14, 2014, ISBN 9781449793890.

BIOGRAPHY

Coincidentally, I am a left-handed writer. As a husband, father, pastor, and a born-again believer of the Lord Jesus Christ with a desire to write about God's Words, the Holy Bible, and how God is working in me; I mean anywhere, anyplace, or anytime; in my car, during church services, traveling to and from hotels, or cottages.

Yes, I use my writing to help spread the Gospel of Christ to the people of the World by inviting them to Christ, rejoicing in the sanctified word of God.

Thank you for allowing me to share my words with you the reader. I have been made glad and blessed, so I feel sure of you that my joy through the Lord Jesus Christ may be the joy of you also.

DEDICATION

As this book is about equipping believers to be remarkably inviters and faithful witnesses, I dedication this publication to my late adored Pastors of my youth:

Rev. E. W. Washington, I want to thank you for being my first pastor and wonderful sermons. It was a refreshing way to hear about the Word of God (flowing line by line and verse by verse from the Holy Bible). I will always remember the Word of God that you pointed out.

Rev. Walter Lee Debro, Sr., I want to thank you for preaching the eternal Word. I believe the Word today because you and the church you led gave me that grounding.

On behalf of *"Witnesses Model - Proclamation of the Gospel,"* I would like to thank you both for all your teachings. This experience has already increased my desire for a never-ending relationship with God.

To those who are displeased and disappointed may this book be an encouragement to you. To those who are busy making things happen, may this book be an encouragement to continue. And to those who are unaware of what's happening, may this book provide as a tool in the appropriate place.

Special Dedication:

A special dedication to Rev. Dr. Arthur Hughes, mentor of my youth, giving me the opportunity to preach my first revival in my small home town. The church revival was extraordinary! I enjoyed it, and it positively impacted my life. Bless you, much appreciated.

PARENTS DEDICATION

      Naturally having great parents is worth more than all the money in the whole world!

      My parents, JW and Sarah Lee Banks gave me freedom to experience the world at a young age. By allowing me to attend college at the School of Visual Arts in New York City. My passed on father carefully taught, "Life is like a row of cotton, for some people, it is easy going all the way through, and for some others, it's difficult." My passed on mother lovingly encouraged me to do mighty things such as write more teaching books.

      My wife's parents, Eddie James Thomas and Dianna Layne both represent the most perfect, loving people you would ever want to meet. I define them — not by how much they are loved, but by how much they love others. My passed on father-in-law said passionately, "Tommy, I'm proud to have you as a son." My lovely mother-in-law sincerely thank you for being more than I ever expected you to be.

      These four people come from different backgrounds, but help me to better understand soul witnessing for Christ.

ACKNOWLEDGMENTS

Thanks To

My only Lord and Savior Jesus Christ for placing His Holy Spirit upon me; yes, it is the love of God that compels me!

My wife and son, Wanda (Lady B) and Tommy Jr., my passed on parents (aka moma em) JW and Sarah, my passed on sister Jeannie, my siblings, my dearest cousin Prophetess Renda Horne, has authored two books entitled, ***"Seven Years in Egypt; Seven Years in Egypt- recognizing your setbacks as set-ups for your comeback,"*** my friends, and to all these people; Mentors, Pastors, Predecessors, Teachers, and Parishioners.

The former Mayor of Como, Mississippi, the Honorable Azria "Bobby" Lewers, thank you for all your support and being a shining example for others to follow. It has always been clear to me that you have sacrificed a lot in service of this community. I end with the two words I started with, they do not begin to express how grateful I am to you, Thank you!

Special Acknowledgments:

A particular thanks to Rev. Dr. Booker T. Sears, Jr. I want to thank you for your message on October 25, 1987. It was a refreshing way to hear about "The Red-eyed Green-eyed Monster" from (First

Samuel chapter 18 and verse 9). "And Saul eyed David from that day and forward."

"Halloween-monsters, goggling ghosts, and modern vampires will all disappear but the old red-eyed green-eyed monster keeps on living every day of the year." I will continue memorizing the message you pointed out. Thanks for being a fabulous pastor.

I appreciate you for all your brotherly love and support; providing me the opportunity to preach the Gospel of Jesus Christ to the congregation and Tuesday's Fellowship Ministry. Bless you, much appreciated.

ABOUT THE BOOK

My conscious purpose of carefully writing this psychological feature book was naturally to help young pastors and members of the Lord's body. To convincingly demonstrate in their dear lives and properly apply in their local churches the biblical concepts of their leading role as faithful witnesses.

I sincerely pray that God will use this precious book to encourage and help you faithfully fulfill the challenging task to be church inviters and moral witnesses.

ABOUT THE AUTHOR

    Tommy has been preaching for more than 35 years. He has faithfully served as beloved pastor of Progressive Baptist Church, Harlem, New York. He has also served as a law enforcement professional; and has received recognition and honor at the police officer's annual awards ceremony in Marshall County. He received the doctor of divinity degree (in Religious Studies) from Tennessee School of Religion Seminary. His doctoral dissertation was titled *"A Study of the Christian Faith of hoping from the Perspective of the way an African American Person or Black Church Thinks."*
    His goal is to help people to be remarkably inviters and faithful witnesses by providing tips, ideas, and examples through books of the Bible or through a large section of Scriptures.

LOOK FOR THESE OTHER BOOKS BY TOMMY R. BANKS, SR.

www.ingramcontent.com/pod-product-compliance
Lightning Source LLC
LaVergne TN
LVHW041539060526
838200LV00037B/1052